AMERICAN NOTES

I0140161

Len Jenkin

BROADWAY PLAY PUBLISHING INC
New York
www.broadwayplaypublishing.com
info@broadwayplaypublishing.com

AMERICAN NOTES
© Copyright 1988 by Len Jenkin

First printing, this edition: June 2015
I S B N: 978-0-88145-616-5

Book design: Marie Donovan
Page make-up: Adobe InDesign
Typeface: Palatino
Printed and bound in the U S A

AMERICAN NOTES was first presented by the New York Shakespeare Festival Public Theater (Joseph Papp, Producer) on 18 February 1988. The cast, and creative contributors were as follows:

MAYOR	Rodney Scott Hudson
CHUCKLES	Olek Krupa
PAULINE	Lauren Tom
FABER	Stephen McHattie
PITCHMAN	Thomas Ikeda
KAREN	Mercedes Ruehl
REPORTER	Andrew Davis
TIM	Jesse Borrego
LINDA	Laura Innes
PROFESSOR	George Bartenieff
Director	Joanne Akalaitis
Scenery	John Arnone
Costumes	David C Woolard
Lighting	Frances Aronson
Associate producer	Jason Steven Cohen

Time: Now

Place: America

Tho' obscur'd, this is the form
of the Angelic land.

William Blake: *America*

(An open field, outskirts of town. An older man sits in the dirt, some food and a bottle alongside him. This is the MAYOR. *A traveller enters, dusty, ragged, having walked a long way. He holds a battered suitcase. This is* CHUCKLES. *He stops, as if unsure which way to go. He hesitantly approaches the* MAYOR.*)*

MAYOR: Bound for somewhere, buddy?

*(*CHUCKLES *nods. He points in one direction, then hesitates, points in another direction. He looks around confusedly.)*

MAYOR: Well, little buddy—stay or walk.

*(*CHUCKLES *moves about uncertainly, stops.)*

MAYOR: You want advice, or directions?

*(*CHUCKLES *stands silent, ill at ease.)*

MAYOR: You want advice. *(He looks* CHUCKLES *over carefully.)* You been travelling, little buddy. Probably looking for it, but you ain't found it yet. Hmmmm... your eyes been sucking up so much world they got swelled up like beachballs, poppin' outta your face. Ooo wee! You know, you keep moving and peeping in everywhichplace, you can raise up a big wind in your head, special if you don't know exactly what you looking at. Why just yesterday I was out taking my constitutional —past the flag go flap flap on the village green, past the newsstand, past a man slicing another man's face with a breadknife, past old Mister and Mrs Whoever's house and she's praying with her thumb up her Bible and he's rubbing his moneymaker, and I stop to take a leak behind the barn and who do I see hailing a cab in the dark but little Miss Muffet, and her hair's all tangled and she ain't walking right. Hey, I seen a guy follow somebody's daughter into the all night launderama and he's got his dick hid inna boxa Tide. I see em go in there and she's folding up her underwear, and I'm looking through the keyhole and all that wash is spinning round and round and round.

I seen a man, 'bout this time yesterday, slit his own throat in the bathroom mirror. Home sweet home, you betcha. Run around to nowhere till they drop, ain't even looking. Am I right?

(CHUCKLES *nods in agreement. He shyly eyes the* MAYOR's *food. The* MAYOR *eyes* CHUCKLES.)

MAYOR: Hey…uh, (*Naming him.*) Chuckles! Chuckles, you want something to eat?

(CHUCKLES *grabs the food, begins to chomp away.*)

MAYOR: Hey…my lunch. You are supposed to leave me something.

(CHUCKLES, *frightened, drops the food quickly, pushes it back over to the* MAYOR. *The* MAYOR, *in turn, places the food carefully back between the two of them.* CHUCKLES *hesitantly takes something to eat. The* MAYOR *nods.*)

MAYOR: Now I been on that road myself. Got tired one day, and settled down. Right here. Got a wife and three kids. Why just last week I got elected mayor. Ain't much in it but I like the honor you know, from my fellow citizens. Nasty and slow as they may be, they got glimmers, glimmers way down in their underpants, know what I mean little buddy. Down there—and in the very center of the eye, in the black dot.

I got a good idea where you're headed. Why you know there's nine rivers between here and there, and you moving like you gonna get there Tuesday. There's the Muskinggum, an' the Chattahoocie, the Raritanic, the Monongahoola, the Gahoolamonga, the Belly-Up, the

Snake, and the Skunk. Whooooooo! You counting?
There's one so fearsome it either doesn't have a name
or I'm scared to tell it. You think this some tiddlywink
country like Alboonia you step outta your shack to
take a piss and if the wind's right you are watering
foreign soil? This is the land of Rootie Kazootie and the
Appaloosa, sea to shining sea. Go somewhere and die!
Whooboy!
You moving on to somewhere cause you think this
ain't it, but you don't know this country or these
people around here, little bitty buddy, so there's
nothing but wind in your head. It's whistling between
your ears, bitty buddy. Just wind. You got your lips
loose yet? No talkee, eh? Wanna wrestle? Wanna swap
socks? *(He conceals his socks with his hands.)* No peeking.
Look in my pocket. Waddaya see?

(The MAYOR *holds open his pants pocket.* CHUCKLES *peers into it.)*

MAYOR: Pocket fulla darkness—hooboy! Hey,
Chuckles, wiggle down in the dirt here.

*(*CHUCKLES *and the* MAYOR *sit on the ground.)*

MAYOR: Hey, eat some more lunch here.

*(*CHUCKLES *eats.)*

MAYOR: Ease your weary mind. This is some place,
all right. You lucky you here. You oughta get work,
stay awhile…I might be able to place a man of your
talents…

(Lights up in another area on PAULINE, *a young woman standing motionless in the center of a motel office.)*

MAYOR: Look around. Hey, see there's Pauline. She
works late…
Hey, Chuckles. Suck up some of this juice I got here …
Made it special for ya…

(MAYOR hands CHUCKLES his bottle, and CHUCKLES drinks.)

MAYOR: …and open your eyes …

(Lights fade on CHUCKLES and MAYOR, come up more strongly on PAULINE. In the motel office, a counter closes a small area off from the rest of the space. Behind the counter, a chair. On the counter, a bell, a register, some books, a small T V, a phone. A radio plays. Out in the space, a few chairs. Through a screen door, the "outside": perhaps a sign reading "OFFICE" with an arrow, parking stripes on cracked asphalt. PAULINE the niteclerk suddenly rushes over to the screen door, opens it, and leans out.)

PAULINE: GET OUT OF HERE! Leave me alone, please! You're drunk, you know that? GO AWAY AND STOP BOTHERING ME! I'm gonna call the police if you don't get outta here, NOW!

(PAULINE goes back behind the desk, reaches for the phone, then changes her mind. She's nervous, listening for any noise. Suddenly the screen door opens. A man enters in a rumpled suit and tie. He goes up to Pauline, and looks at her expectantly.)

FABER: I'm in 4. I left my key.

PAULINE: Oh…yeah.

(PAULINE hands FABER his key.)

FABER: Thanks. Good night. *(He heads for the door, but her voice stops him.)*

PAULINE: Uh, excuse me. Mister Faber?

FABER: How'd you know my name?

PAULINE: It's in the register. Room 4.

FABER: Right. I've never seen you here before.

PAULINE: I'm the niteclerk. I don't come in till twelve, so if you don't stay out late, or get up early, you don't see me.

FABER: Uh, right. Good night, miss...

PAULINE: Pauline. Mister Faber, did you see anyone hanging around on your way in?

FABER: Not a soul, Pauline.

PAULINE. Would you mind doing me a favor? Could you go outside and take a look around the parking lot?

FABER: I'll play. What am I looking for?

PAULINE: There's this drunk guy who's been hanging around here bothering me, and I think he's gone now, but I'm not sure...

(FABER *hesitates, then shrugs his shoulders.*)

FABER: O K. I'll take a look.

(FABER *Exits.* PAULINE *waits nervously. Lights up in another area on an older man, the* PITCHMAN, *in front of an enclosure with a curtained entrance. Some carnival lights. A huge painted banner depicts the lush landscape of Egypt, the pyramids, and the river Nile. The* PITCHMAN *is seated on a stool. He has a microphone. Near him stands* CHUCKLES, *who has a container half full of water in his hands.*)

PITCHMAN: *(On mike)* Come in and see the crocodile, Papa Crocodile, the biggest, oldest, mightiest of them all. Man killer. Swamp monster. Alive on the inside. Listen to him kick and splash. Sounds like he's coming out of there... *(Looks at* CHUCKLES*)* ...sounds like he's coming OUTTA THERE!

(CHUCKLES *shakes his container, making a splashing sound near the mike.*)

PITCHMAN: From the land of the pharaohs, the sphinx and the pyramids comes the crocodile, the colossus of reptiles, twelve hundred pounds of tail lashing, jaw

gnashing danger. Bonecrusher! See him now. Listen
to him thrash about in there. Sounds like he's about to
come outta there, doesn't it?

(CHUCKLES *splashes.*)

PITCHMAN: No danger at all. You'll be separated from
him by two sets of steel bars. Go right in. The show is
always open. Go right in...

(From a distance, a man's voice, screaming)

MAN'S VOICE: Pauline!

(The PITCHMAN *pauses a moment, then continues.)*

PITCHMAN: See Bonecrusher, the summum bonum of
nature's awesome power and cruelty, etcetera, etcetera
and so forth. That's the pitch, which is one thing. The
attraction's another. Some shows, what's on the inside
ain't worth spitting at. Crusher's the real thing. You
got the real thing, people come. Even in Boobopolis,
or Chump Junction, or Hayseed Center, or wherever
the fuck we are this week. People go on in and tell me,
Mister, you didn't say enough, and come back with the
family.
See Bone-crusher, the monster of the Nile, alive on the
inside. No sir, this is not a movie. Alive!

*(*CHUCKLES *and the* PITCHMAN *are still, as lights on them
fade out. In the motel office area,* FABER *returns.)*

FABER: There was this guy leaning over the one car
in the parking lot...mine. He's vomiting on the hood.
So I say, "uh, buddy, get off my car," and he heaves
again and then he turns around to me with puke all
over his football jersey and he says "You're the one."
I do believe he thought I was your boyfriend. I was
flattered. I figured I wouldn't disillusion him. I say "I
am the one. Go—and be sick somewhere else."

PAULINE: Did he?

FABER: First he took a swing at me. He missed, and he falls down and sort of crawls away. Then he stands up and he howls.

MAN'S VOICE: *(Off stage)* Pauline!

FABER: You probably heard that part. Then he just wanders off into the dark. I see him again when he hits the highway light near the junction, and he bobs and weaves a bit under the light, and he's gone. He the town wino? Or a lover you won't see no more?

PAULINE: Just some guy.

(FABER takes a seat.)

FABER: Hey…you want a favor, and I don't even know you, and I go to shoo this guy away. He's mean drunk, bigger than me, and could have been carrying the kitchen cleaver. I take my life in my hands out there, and you won't answer a little question to help me pass the time.

PAULINE: It's true, what I said. He's just some guy.

FABER: No. That's me. I'm just some guy. I'm staying here, you never saw me before, you say hello cause that's your job, and I'm gone. He's somebody. He's got a name. He may even have a mother. Right in town… that's where he's going now. Home, and his Moms is sitting in the kitchen in a flower print nightdress, waiting up. Radio's on, some kinda endless traffic report. She's reading the back of a box of Fab, and when he hits the screen door, she looks up. "Where you been, Bobby? Your hair's all tangled and you ain't talking right. Oooh wee you got puke and blood all over you…"

PAULINE: Blood? He's got blood all over him?

FABER: Thought I'd leave out that part. I kicked him.

PAULINE: You kicked him? I asked you to look around, not to kick him or something. Why'd you do that? Oh Jesus, why .

FABER: I kicked him cause he was lying on the asphalt and he says "goddamn cunt I'm going back there and fuck her up." He said something along those lines. So I kicked him in the face. He bled a little. Discouraging him seemed like a good idea at the time. You got someone who can stay with you for a few nights till he cools off? Hell, he'll probably be back with a shotgun .

PAULINE: You're kidding, aren't you? I hope…

FABER: Yeah. He's gone. Who is he?

PAULINE: Nobody. I teach exercise twice a week, in town. The studio has a window on the street, so it's kind of advertising, but anyone can just look in and see us jumping around in leotards. One day, there's this guy I never saw before, and he watches the whole fifty-five minutes, like he's hypnotized. Next day he comes inside and says he wants to sign up. I tell him the class is full. That was a lie, and I didn't like saying it, but there's something funny about him, like he's not seeing what's there, but something else he likes better—but you're not too sure you'd like it better—and he's seeing it all the time. Then he asks me out. I had to get Elaine to make him leave. Then he showed up here tonight. He was drunk. I was scared. Thanks for helping me out.

FABER: He got caught by something is all. Your hair, some angle of your body, something in your face locked in to a dream of his and he grabbed at it only way he had. He'll forget it—till some other time and place—somebody else in a window tilts her head a certain way, and the rusted old gears mesh, and he once more presses his nose against the glass. It's a great life. What time is it?

PAULINE: After two.

FABER: I'm wide awake.

PAULINE: Me, too. You want some coffee? I've got a hot plate in the back, and some instant…

FABER: Yeah…that's good. That's fine. I like that.

PAULINE: O K.

(PAULINE *exits through a rear door behind the desk.* FABER *alone.* CHUCKLES *enters. He carries a vacuum cleaner. He stares suspiciously at* FABER. *He exits.*)

FABER. (*Calling offstage*) Hey, am I the only one staying here? Tonight, I mean.

PAULINE: (*From off*) Well, we really have only one other guest. Another single. God, she's real beautiful. Hasn't been out of her room for three days. She's been calling over, though, for messages.

FABER: Yeah?

(PAULINE *returns with two coffee cups and a jar of powdered cream. She sets them down on the counter.*)

PAULINE: I got Cremora, the powder?

FABER: That's fine. Uh…

(FABER *gets up and goes over to* PAULINE, *who is behind her desk.*)

FABER: I got a bottle of whiskey here in one pocket, unopened. Maybe we just adulterate the coffee a little. What do you think, Pauline?

PAULINE: O K, but just a little for me. I've gotta work till eight.

FABER: I know. You're on the job, Pauline. (*He adds whiskey to the coffee.*) If I ring the bell, you'll ask what you can do for me. (*He rings the bell. Silence for a moment.*)

PAULINE: Mister Faber, where've you been tonight? I know you didn't take your car cause it's been sitting there since I came on, so I thought hey, Mister Faber in 4 must have friends in town. After all, he's been here a week, and what else is there to stay around here that long for?

FABER: Pauline, I bet you figure out a lot of things, don't you?

PAULINE: I bet it's a girlfriend. She's got a car, and picked you up, and you…

FABER: You got this one wrong. I don't know anyone anywhere near here. I was out walking. In town.

PAULINE: Everything's closed.

FABER: I wasn't shopping. I was walking. So, Pauline. What do you do here all night long?

PAULINE: Homework, mostly. I got an English lit assignment for tomorrow. I just started, part time. At the community college, out on 119. It's going O K so far.

FABER: Sounds like something, I guess…

PAULINE: All my friends went to college a year ago. But my mom wouldn't have the county nurse before.

FABER: Mind if I ask just what you're talking about?

PAULINE: Oh…sorry. My mom's not real well, and someone's gotta be around her almost all the time. Now, the nurse is there, and I can work this job, and start school.

FABER: Uh, Pauline, long as we're having this coffee and all, I'd feel better if you just came out from behind the desk, and we'd just sit around here like people do, you know.

PAULINE: I'm not supposed to be out there where the guests sit.

FABER: We're not gonna be having any more company tonight.

(PAULINE *comes hesitantly out from behind the desk, sits in a chair by* FABER. *They drink coffee.*)

FABER: Now, uh, Pauline, are you single?

PAULINE: Sure. I told you. I live with my Mom.

FABER: Well, for all I knew your husband was living there too, and the two of you had a little room up in the attic where you baked brownies or something, ran the volunteer fire department, a little palmistry scam… and then the two of you being real quiet till your Mom goes off to sleep, then once you hear the sick old lady snoring you leap at each other, tearing…

PAULINE: No. Just me and my mom.

FABER: Let me make a comment here, Pauline. I was downtown there in the downtown tonight, and it seemed as if someone had pressed the pause button on the whole neighborhood around 1942. Quiet. Sort of permanently still. Awful slow for actual people. And out here, right now, even stranger. No wind, no traffic…I can hear the breath going in and out of you.

PAULINE: I think that's your own breath you're hearing, Mister Faber.

FABER: Yeah, You're right. That's what it is.

PAULINE: I'm gonna get to my book for awhile, O K?

FABER: You don't mind if I sit up here a bit?

PAULINE: Make yourself at home. There's nobody here but us…

(*Phone rings.*)

PAULINE: …and the girl in 7.

(PAULINE *picks up the desk phone. Lights up in a room of the same motel. A stocking hangs out of a suitcase on a stand. Empty liquor bottles. A girl in a slip,* KAREN, *is sitting on an unmade bed, the phone in her hand.)*

PAULINE: Office. Can I help you?

KAREN: Yeah, uh Jenny…

PAULINE: Pauline.

KAREN: Oh. Yeah. Pauline, the nite clerk. Listen, Pauline, what time you got?

PAULINE: Exactly… *(Looks at watch)* …2:45.

KAREN: Zat daylight savings or what? Just kidding… Uh, anything for me?

PAULINE: Uh, I'm sorry. No messages.

KAREN: Thanks.

PAULINE: It's no trouble. Good night.

*(*PAULINE *hangs up the phone, as does* KAREN; *to* FABER.*)*

PAULINE: The girl who's waiting…

*(*PAULINE *reads.* FABER *sits quietly. In her room, we hear* KAREN *in V O or live, as indicated. She looks down at a cigarette burnhole in the bedspread.)*

KAREN: *(V O)* Oh Jesus, Karen darling. Look at that. You coulda set your bed on fire. *(She looks around the room. V O)* Musta been a helluva party. I hope I had a good time. Hell, nobody else showed up… *(She opens a liquor bottle, pours a drink, shakes out two aspirin. Live)* Well, onward Christian soldiers. *(She takes the aspirin with a liquor chaser.)* Ugh. What's the worst? He got hit by a truck or something and he's laid up in a hospital, and his face is all bandaged so he can't call. Or, he's dead, so he can't call. *(V O)* You'd almost like that Karen darling, cause what's likely is that bastard's out on the road somewhere and he forgot you. You just went right out of his head. "Karen? Who the fuck is that? I don't remember." *(Live)* No. That's not fucking possible. I can tell.

(The REPORTER KAREN'S *waiting for appears in another space. He holds a letter from the* PROFESSOR.*)*

REPORTER: Hey, I've been in heaven for two days, and I am not about to walk away from it and not come back. It's a three hour drive, I'm only gonna be with the guy an hour maybe, tops. Just to take some pictures and notes for the story.

KAREN: *(Live)* You know it's four miles to town, Chump Junction or whatever, only shoes I got are these heels, I got about seventy-five cents in my purse, half a pack of Pall Malls, some groceries, and a bottle of vodka. What am I gonna do here?

REPORTER: How should I know? Read a magazine. Watch the T V. They got T V in the rooms.

KAREN. *(Live)* This professor you're gonna see…he got a phone number?

REPORTER: *(Checking the letter)* Baby, he lives in the middle of god-forsaken nowhere. He doesn't have a phone. I think he doesn't believe in 'em.

(Lights come up on the PROFESSOR *in his farmhouse. A door with many locks, boards nailed over windows, piles of disorganized books, odd electronic equipment, complex charts and diagrams. Perhaps strange atonal music plays. He addresses the audience. In his own space, the* REPORTER *looks over the letter his magazine's received.)*

PROFESSOR: There exist particular spiritual beings who hold certain information invaluable to humanity. In this place, I have entered into unrestrained dialogue with these beings on a variety of congenial topics. To accomplish this, of course, I've had to probe some rather isolated spiritual neighborhoods, previously accessible only by psychic helicopter…

I wrote to the newspapers, magazines, learned societies. Only one response—from a publication mired in lurid speculation and unsubstantiated horseshit. Flying Saucer News.

REPORTER: *(To* KAREN*)* Hey…see ya' in a I'll bit, hah… late tonight or tomorrow. Or tomorrow. Or tomorrow. *(Lights strong on* KAREN, *the* PROFESSOR, *the* REPORTER. *A knock on the* PROFESSOR'*s door. He opens it warily.* CHUCKLES *enters, bringing the* PROFESSOR *some take-out food. He eats ravenously, as* CHUCKLES *listens.)*

PROFESSOR: These beings, these shadow people, they're around us, all the time. They can't fly, or raise the dead, or control the weather. They're very light, you know. The wind can blow them away, if they're not careful. Very light. Very beautiful.

*(*CHUCKLES *Exits. The* PROFESSOR *locks the door, continues.)*

PROFESSOR: Some say they've always existed, and will exist forever. I wouldn't say that. Some say they are the dead. I wouldn't say that. They're just there, alongside us, like feelings in the air.

(Lights down on the PROFESSOR.*)*

KAREN: *(Live)* Three days in this hole. What day is it anyway? V O) Maybe it's Sunday, and I should go to church or something.

*(*KAREN *picks up the phone, dials. In the motel office, it rings.)*

PAULINE: Office.

KAREN: Hey, Pauline, what day you got?

PAULINE: It's Monday now.

KAREN: Any messages?

PAULINE: Nothing yet. Sorry.

KAREN: Thanks.

(KAREN and PAULINE hang up the phones.)

KAREN: *(V O)* On the way over to the motel he says let's get you some groceries to take up to the room. I say O K and we pull up at the 7-11 and on the way in I trip over a fucking tricycle some kid leaves there in front of the door. I ripped my stocking on the pedal. I guess I'm nervous or something cause I start kicking the bike. The kid comes rushing out, screaming at me. He's got a big container of purple snow in his hand. *(Live)* The place's microwave is busted. He buys me a frozen burrito and tells me it'll thaw, and an orange soda and a beer and some kinda dead french fries, all gonna taste like cardboard puke. He pays, and he hands the whole bag to me like it's fulla gold, with this shiteating grin on his face. I smile back and say hey whyn't you just leave me fifty bucks and I'll get my own groceries… *(V O)* I could see I said the wrong thing. He'd been burned before. He just looked over my shoulder at a shelf full of motor oil. Forget it, 1 say, I don't need no money. You're gonna be back tomorrow, right? And I give him a kiss, a nice wet one with a little tongue in it. He smiles. *(Live)* What a chump. *(V O)* "Day after, the latest," he says…and he drops me here and he's gone. Frozen burrito and an orange soda. Purple snow.

REPORTER: See ya in a l'il bit, hah…late tonight. Or tomorrow. *(Exits)*

KAREN: *(Live)* Hey, anything coulda happened. Car broke down. Couldn't find that professor. Maybe he forgot the name of this place so he couldn't call. Hey, Karen darling. Believe. He'll be here…

(Lights up on the same PITCHMAN we've seen before, in front of the same crocodile exhibit: banner, entranceway in to see the crocodile. Near the enclosure is CHUCKLES. He holds

*the closed container of water, the splasher. He shakes his
container. Sound of splashing)*

PITCHMAN: *(On mike)* No, sir, it is not a movie. Alive
on the inside. Bonecrusher, world's largest... Hey,
Chuckles. Wet Mister B down, will ya?

CHUCKLES: Splushh splush?

PITCHMAN: Yeah.

CHUCKLES: Splush splush! Splish!

*(*CHUCKLES *goes into the crocodile's enclosure. An attractive
young girl and her boyfriend walk up to the exhibit. This is*
LINDA *and* TIM.*)*

TIM: *(To* PITCHMAN*)* Hi! My name's Tim. This is Linda.
Linda, say hello to the nice man.

LINDA: Hello.

TIM: We want to see, uh, Bonecrusher, you call him?

PITCHMAN: That's what I call him, and that's his name.
His Momma gave it to him on the banks of the Nile,
in Crocodilopolis. Enter and discover. Or you can go
downtown to Penny's and watch the wax dummies in
the window.

*(*LINDA *and* TIM *disappear into Bonecrusher's enclosure.
The* PITCHMAN*'s eyes follow* LINDA *as they exit. He turns
to the audience.)*

PITCHMAN: You know what age is to me? It's a number.
Sixty. Nineteen. Zero. That's all the fuck it is, a fucking
number. Hey, couple of local girls come around
wearing these shorts show half their ass when they
lean over to look at Bonecrusher, and he ain't looking
at them but I am and they say, Hey, how you doing,
Pop? You want some of that, Pop? Hey, my name's
Marty, cut that Pop crap, you know. Now I ain't saying
it's exactly the same. If she tries to gimme a blow job

every ten minutes I'm gonna say hey what you doing you trying to kill me or something.

Been with Bonecrusher for thirty years. Got him when I got outta the army in '58. Hey, I'm different, he's the same, but that's on the outside. Inside, I'm just like him—no change at all.

That's Chuckles. Found him wandering around the lot when we hit town. I taught him how to hose out the cage, do some other little stuff around here. Boss wanted to throw him off the lot, I said, hey, no way, Chuckles stays with me. Cause I had an idea. I treat him good, feed him, let him sleep under the drop here. It's next to Crusher, and sometimes it don't smell all that good, but he don't mind. We got a deal, Chuckles and me. Chuckles is gonna feed me to Crusher when I die. I needed an idiot. Nobody else would do it. When I found Chuckles, I knew I found my boy. I'm a religious man, in my way. If Bonecrusher eats me, I'll go on living, looking out of his eyes. You'll be able to see me in there, a little spark of red fire way back in those black slits of nothing. Hey, I'll be him, and he'll be me. Bullshit spook stuff, hah? I don't care what you think. Sense to me don't gotta be sense to you.

Listen and learn. What you think ain't all the thinking there is. Bonecrusher is a priest. It's all in Job, and I got it by heart.
Canst thou draw out Leviathan with a hook?
Who can open the doors of his face? Or
light the lamps of his mouth? Will he
speak soft words unto thee? Will he make
a covenant with thee? Will he take thee for
a servant forever? Upon earth there is not
his like, who is made without fear. He
beholdeth all high things, and sorrow is
turned into joy before him.

*(*LINDA *and* TIM *emerge from Bonecrusher's enclosure.)*

TIM: Hey, fella. I hate to tell you this, but your croc's dead.

PITCHMAN: You don't say. *(Laughs)* You know anything about crocodiles, friend? They look deader'n hell most of the time.

TIM: Excuse me, but that animal in there is gone, finished.

PITCHMAN: That's Bonecrusher in there, and he'll outlive you or me.

TIM: He's dead. Probably been dead for a week.

PITCHMAN: Fuck you and your mother, friend. Chuckles!

*(*CHUCKLES *advances, as menacingly as he can manage, toward* TIM. TIM *grabs him suddenly, twists, and* CHUCKLES *is on his knees.)*

TIM: *(To* PITCHMAN*)* You're right about one thing. He is big. But he's not Egyptian, and he's not a crocodile. He's an American alligator. Do you want to sell the body?

LINDA: Bury him, or put him in the town dump where the birds'll strip him clean. Children can play with his bones.

*(*LINDA *and* TIM *exit, and from off, their laughter.)*

PITCHMAN: Chuckles, go in there and poke Mister B.

*(*CHUCKLES *enters the croc's enclosure. A moment later, he slowly emerges. He looks down at the ground.)*

PITCHMAN: I been with him thirty years, Chuckles. I been on the road with him every season. I got repeat customers. These people bring their kids. Little god-damn kids. Know how he got so big, sonny? People think he grew fat on fear. That's not so. He's big with love... *(He sits down again in his usual position, in front of the huge banner. He picks up his microphone.)* See Bone-crusher, World's Largest Crocodile, Colossus of reptiles, monster of the Nile. Hear him splash around in there. I do believe he's coming out of there...

*(*CHUCKLES *makes shaking motions, but his hands are empty. No splashing sound)*

PITCHMAN: No sir, this is not a movie. Alive on the inside. *(To* CHUCKLES*)* Bonecrusher ain't dead, Chuckles. He's sleeping, that's all. Needs his rest. After all the horrible things he's done his whole life long, he needs his rest...

*(*CHUCKLES *and the* PITCHMAN *are still. In the motel office,* PAULINE *reads.* FABER *sits quietly.)*

FABER: Pauline?

PAULINE: Yes, Mister Faber?

FABER: Pauline, now that we're sitting around here together and all—would you tell me a story?

PAULINE: I don't know any stories.

FABER: You already told me one, Pauline. About the exercise class.

PAULINE: That wasn't a story, Mister Faber. It happened.

FABER: Story all the same, Pauline. Just like when some old lady comes down in her pajamas says Pauline honey I can't get a wink so give a listen to my life. It's the same as all the others so I guess the joke's on me. You could read it on line at the supermarket, hear ern shout it over the cornfields, but hey—hear it now, 'cause what you the nite-clerk for anyway? Tell me that one, Pauline, and when you're done I'll comment, and we'll be having a conversation here.

PAULINE: I can't tell you a story, Mister Faber. Not just
like that, anyway.

FABER: All right, then I'll tell you one, Pauline. All you
got to do is listen.

*(Lights up on a bar somewhere. Over the bar, a T V plays:
picture, no sound. There's also a pinball machine, and a
small stage at the rear. On that stage, LINDA and TIM,
a performing duo. They do a song, perhaps their version
of Sonny and Cher's I Got You, Babe. During the song,
FABER enters, and sits at the bar.)*

*(From the motel office, PAULINE watches. The song ends,
and LINDA goes to pinball, plays. TIM comes over to FABER.)*

TIM: My name's Tim. I'm living at the hotel. Blaine
Hotel right up the street. Hey, after the accident, before
I had this job, I was working polishing airport floors in
the middle of the night. It's quiet, and I liked the way
the machine kept humming. If I stuck six months they
were gonna embroider my name on my uniform. TIM.
I left. Airport's for the planes really, not the people,
you know. Got this job, took a room right up the street.
Come over and see me. I could put you so straight
you wouldn't bend again for days—years, maybe.
(Pointing.) That's Linda. Linda, say hello to the nice
man.

LINDA: Hello.

TIM: You know why Linda stays with me?

FABER: I…

TIM: Cause she's crazy, that's why. Besides, she's on
the four to twelve shift at Denny's out on Arctic, and
when she's done, she needs somebody to love.
I flatter myself. Listen, buddy. The truth is she sleeps
on the floor with her clothes on, in the bathroom next
to the tub, curled up in an old army blanket I got. I
lay there in bed and I whisper and I say Linda Linda

come on into bed here. It's warm and I took a bath
before I got in, and the sheets is clean, and I ain't gonna
do nothing—I'm just gonna hold you. I say all that
whispering loud so she'll hear me in the bathroom, but
she never answers. I never know if she hears me, or if
she's sleeping. When I say that stuff to her I ain't lying,
you know. I ain't lying, but I'm hoping…
Listen, Bob. You know Linda got two kids. Would you
believe it? Yeah, they live in Reno, Nevada. She lost
'em on a bet. Now she's here.
You like her, Bob? She got very nice tits. Not saggy at
all, you know. She's like a girl in a magazine—not a
mark on her. Clean and healthy. And she don't think
about anything. Not much anyway. Not anymore.
Listen to me, Bob. You got nothing, right? You got
a rented room, you got a momma somewhere if she
ain't dead, you got what's inside you head, which
by peeking in through your eyes, those transparent
windows of the soul, I can see ain't much. You have
fallen through an American crack, and them is deep.
Whole damn country is mined with 'em, it's like
walking over quicksand, open up and swallow a
young man quick as say howdy want some pancakes.
You got trouble. Trouble is my experteeze. I majored in
trouble at a major university. We are talking English,
capish? Comprendo? This isn't sound. This is the
straight skinny, no tricks, no figure it out later, no get
it in your dreams. This is get it now and take it home.
Me and Linda are here. That's fortuitous. Good graces
is what you're in, friend. God loves you, and I could
learn. So could Linda.

FABER: What makes you think you can come over here
and say all this shit to me?

TIM: I gotta license. You wanna see it?

FABER: Do you think I'm stupid? That I'm gonna let the two of you just take my…

TIM: No. You're not stupid. You had some bad luck is all. Scuse me, buddy. Look her over whiles I take a dump. I'll be back with ya shortly.

(TIM *exits into the bathroom.* LINDA *comes over and sits with* FABER.)

LINDA: Hello.

FABER: Hello. You, uh, come from around here?

LINDA: Sure. Sure I do. Right around here. I come from right here.

FABER: What do you do? I mean, what do you do? You work?

LINDA: I am intending to get work, so I can fuck who I like. (*Pointing to the stage*) I sing here for the hell of it. It doesn't pay. As they say, poverty sucks, but then, employment ain't much better. That's a bind, Mister.

FABER: Where do you live?

LINDA: With Timmy. But it's filthy. I have plans to get ahold of some amphetamines, and take 'em with a broom and a box of brillo nearby. Timmy's nuts, you know. He's here somewhere, 'less he left. He knows I can find my way back, so he doesn't have to stay, you know.

(CHUCKLES *enters, goes behind the bar, where he seems to work. He listens.*)

LINDA: You know what love can do? Rip you to shit, then come upside your head with a two by four and knock what's left of you right into the street. Think so?

FABER: Yeah. I know so.

LINDA: Everything Tim told you about me is a bunch of lying shit. You know that?

FABER: I…

LINDA: I mean, he thinks I exist only for him. When I go out into the hallway and slam the door behind me, he thinks I dissolve in the corridor before I get to the stairs. I reconstitute myself a moment before I come into his presence. Now you know that's not true, cause I'm here, and he's not…aren't I?

FABER: Yeah, you are.

LINDA: Touch me so you're sure.

FABER: I'm sure.

LINDA: Touch me, dammit.

(FABER *touches* LINDA.)

FABER: Your hand is hot.

LINDA: No. Yours is cold. You're freezing. You're going below zero, with the negative numbers. You wanna buy me a drink?

FABER: Sure.

LINDA: (*To* CHUCKLES) I'll have a shot of Wild Turkey, black coffee, and a glass of water, please.

(CHUCKLES *looks around confusedly behind the bar to fill her order. To* FABER.)

LINDA: Do I have lipstick on my teeth?

FABER: As a matter of fact, yeah. A little.

LINDA: Would you wipe it off? Use your finger.

(FABER *does so. She catches his finger in her mouth, sucks on it gently, then suddenly bites hard. He leaps away.*)

FABER: Owww!

(TIM *opens the men's room door, heads toward them.*)

TIM: She's cute. Don't pay any attention to her now, Bob. She's not yours yet. No deal yet. Listen to me. You're here for a reason, right? You're a man in need.

Am I right? I mean, you can tell me, us, you can
tell us because we are nothing but need. We desire
everything. You name it, we want it, and we want it
bad.

Hey, I'm talking to you buddy. Hey, I'm asking you a
question.

FABER: I wasn't listening.

TIM: Some people think their ears just hang there
and work all by themselves. You know a smart guy
can take his ears off and put 'em in his pocket in
Guatemala or something. But that don't matter, Bob,
cause you're full of shit on this one, and I say that
with conviction. You were straining to hear me, like a
kid can't take a shit. You been hearing every mother-
fucking word. Well?

FABER: I want her.

TIM: (*Laughs*) You know, Bob, you and me we're gonna
be friends. In fact, Bob, we're friends right now. What's
your name? Shhhh. Don't tell me. What's a little name
between friends.

What's your offer? You keep sleeping alone, friend,
you die inside. What you can buy by the hour ain't
worth the chump change you lay out for it. That is not
heat to warm you. You are a man who can smell true
love when it's coming down the street, you can smell
it coming to you cross the rivers and seas, its odor
mixing with the salt spray and the quick perfume of
the flying fish. You know it when it's sitting right here
alongside you.

Gimme something. For Linda. All you got. She's worth
it...

(*A long silence.* FABER *doesn't move or speak.*)

TIM: You wanna play, but you don't wanna pay. This
is true of everyone. The piper will pipe till the gates of

dawn, drag your dancing body along, but you gotta pay at the end of the road. *(Sings)* "I ain't the devil or the devil's son, but I can be the devil till the devil come..." Well? After tonight, I won't be around to fix you.

FABER: No deal.

TIM: Well, whaddaya know. Bright boy, maybe. Might not have worked out too well for you, in the long run. I coulda pressed you harder—but hell, why hook you? Maybe you'll meet me again someday, and I don't want no bad blood between us. I surely don't. Come on, Linda. Let's go.

(LINDA *and* TIM *exit.* FABER *sits alone, then crosses to* PAULINE *in the motel office as lights fade in the bar.)*

FABER: *(To* PAULINE*)* Funny, hah? What do you think, Pauline?

PAULINE: I don't know, Mister Faber. What do you think?

FABER: I think they were extremely quick. Everytime they threw me one I fumbled, tripped, and fell over in the grass. They had me looking like Mexican money— with holes in it. They let me off easy.

(A moment's silence)

PAULINE: Mister Faber, would you ever think about living here?

FABER: In the motel? Sure. Forever.

PAULINE: You know what I mean. It's not as slow here as it looks. Things happen, but kind of one at a time, like... Are you interested in this?

FABER: It's not really coming through at the moment, Pauline. Maybe you should try something else.

PAULINE: O K... You know the high school a few miles down the road? Around this time of year we bring in a carnival, the V F W does it actually, and they move right onto the football field. It might be there right now.

FABER: So?

PAULINE: What do you mean, so?

FABER: So, what, uh, follows?

PAULINE: Nothing. Just a story.

FABER: Pauline, you gotta be more interesting. I mean to press this point here. Don't you wanna do things, or make things, or be what you read about in books, or see on your T V there? I mean, you could get where you feel O K cause you do this or that and other people think it's hot shit. Hey, keep humping back there behind the desk and you gonna turn into a zombie, Pauline. This place gonna be the Zombieland Motel. Tourists welcome.

PAULINE: What do you think I should do? I'm happy here, Mister Faber, I think. I'm hardly ever bored. I got so many things I…

FABER: That's cause you got a T V there, Pauline, for when you kind of hit a heavy patch of nothing.

PAULINE: I don't want to have an argument with you. Sure, sometimes I watch the late…

FABER: T V's a little strange, isn't it? A tiny, lit-up, twisted replica of everything, that's trying to eliminate our world, and take its place.

PAULINE: Mister Faber, you probably never worked nights. The TV helps pass the time.

(*Silence.* CHUCKLES *enters, cleaning.*)

FABER: I been meaning to ask you. Who's that?

PAULINE: Him? He's just some guy. *(She laughs.)* That's Chuckles. He works around the place. He sleeps here somewhere, nobody really knows where.

FABER: Chuckles, hah?

PAULINE: Someone named him that. He doesn't talk. Except to say the motel motto. I think the owner taught him. Chuckles! The motto!

CHUCKLES: *(In a panic, articulating as best he can.)* We're easy to get to, but hard to leave. *(He exits.)*

PAULINE: We're easy to get to, but hard to leave. You like the coffee?

FABER: Yeah. Uh, you like the whiskey I put in it?

PAULINE: Yeah, warms you up.

FABER: Have some more, Pauline.

PAULINE: O K. But just a bit…

(FABER pours.)

PAULINE: Do you have someone, Mister Faber? You know, like a wife. Or a girlfriend. You know… someone.

FABER: You ask a lot of questions, Pauline.

PAULINE: I'm just curious. It's the only way you can find things out.

FABER: I had someone. About a year ago she left me, her and the kid and everything. I came in late one night, and I'd had a few, and I crawled into bed alongside her, and I'm out. Next thing I knew I hear a crash, open one eye, clock says six A M. I get up and go into the front room, and there she is with her girlfriend Myra, and the kid is already in Myra's old Chevy, and so is all their clothes and stuff, but they can't get the kid's crib through the front door. It was their trying that woke me. I'm standing there naked, looking at her like a dying calf in a hailstorm, and she doesn't even blink. She bends over the crib again and tries to force it through. I wasn't mad. I felt funny and sad seeing her do that. It made me see how she saw me, you know, and that wasn't pretty, but it wasn't true. I walked over to the door, and sat down next to the crib and started taking it apart. Only took ten minutes. Once I did it, she got it out of there and was gone. She didn't even say thank you. She wouldn't even let the kid kiss me goodbye.

I saw her a few times after that, but it was like seeing someone else. So after a while, I just got up and left there. I had the car, and some money, so like I say, I just left. You think I did right, Pauline?

PAULINE: I don't know, Mister Faber. I don't even know you.

FABER: Good as anyone, Pauline.

PAULINE: I couldn't tell if…

FABER: I been here a week, Pauline, cause I don't know whether to go. Or where.

I got money. You want some money? How much would you like?

PAULINE: I can't take your money.

FABER: I'm serious here, Pauline. No difference to me if it's in my pocket or not. Either way, something's gonna happen. Take it all. (*He takes out all his money, including change, and dumps it on* PAULINE's *desk.*)

PAULINE: Mister Faber! Stop! I wouldn't take any money from you, unless I earned it or something.

FABER: You already did that, Pauline.

PAULINE: Coffee's only fifty cents, Mister Faber, and this one was on the house.

FABER: I don't mean the coffee, Pauline.

PAULINE: I know what you mean. Take back your money.

(FABER *takes up the money, puts it back in his pockets.*)

PAULINE: You're probably forgetting a lot of things, Mister Faber.

FABER: I'm remembering a lot, Pauline.

PAULINE: I think you're forgetting.

FABER: You know more about me than me, Pauline? Are we having an argument here?

PAULINE: I wouldn't call it that.

FABER: What would you call it?

(*A long silence between* FABER *and* PAULINE.)

PAULINE: You know what? I don't know why I think this, but I do. I think, even after all you told me, that somehow you're a lucky person.

FABER: You do? Well, maybe I am. Then I don't have to worry, do I? Cause if my luck holds, pretty soon someone's bound to come up behind me and slit my throat.

PAULINE: There's not a lot to say to that, is there? Except that I hope it doesn't happen.

FABER: Do you?

PAULINE: Yes, Mister Faber, I do. (*Silence. She picks up a book, reads. More silence. Then…*) What are doges?

FABER: Doges? What are you doing, the crossword puzzle?

PAULINE: I got a poem to read for my lit class. It's a word in the poem.

FABER: I don't know.

PAULINE: They surrender.

FABER: Who?

PAULINE: The doges. Doges surrender.

FABER: Let's hear it, Pauline.

PAULINE: What?

FABER: The poem.

PAULINE: Safe in their alabaster chambers
Untouched by morning and untouched by Noon
Lie the meek members of the resurrection
Rafter of satin, and roof of stone. More?

FABER: Yeah. The doges didn't come in yet.

PAULINE:
Grand go the years in the crescent above them
Worlds scoop their arcs and firmaments row
Diadems drop, and doges surrender
Soundless as dots on a disc of snow.

FABER: Yeah.

PAULINE: You like it?

FABER: Yeah. I like it. I like you reading it.

PAULINE: What about the doges?

FABER: Not a clue, Pauline. It's a mystery.

(Long silence. The phone rings. PAULINE *picks it up.)*

PAULINE: Office.

(Lights up on KAREN *in her room. She's on the phone.)*

KAREN: Hey, Pauline, what time you got?

PAULINE: About…three A M.

KAREN: Three A M? Are these nights getting longer or what?

PAULINE: I don't know.

KAREN: Me neither… Long as I got you here, why don't you give me my messages. Reel 'em off.

PAULINE: I'm afraid there…

KAREN: Please don't sound so damn sorry.

(KAREN *hangs up her phone, and* PAULINE *follows suit.*
Lights fade on KAREN, FABER, *and* PAULINE *as they come*
up on CHUCKLES *and the* MAYOR *at the* MAYOR'*s place*
in the field near town. CHUCKLES *is sitting in the dirt,*
listening.)

MAYOR. A mayor's got a lot of responsibilities
here, bitty buddy. You think I can put in time on
cartography and transportation for every travelling
boy comes through looking for whereelse and
wherever? I got duties, bitty buddy. Duties. I got to
shave every three days. I got to think about everybody
all at once, including dead people, plus perambulations
and looking around in present time so everybody
round here can step sweetly into the future foot by
foot, which they do every day thank you to God, good
fortune, and the help of a few little doings I do here
and there. The point is, Chuckles, my boy, we walk a
fine line—between yesterday and tomorrow, between
nothing and nothing. You can step right off the log.
We don't wanna go down in flames here, do we bitty
buddy?
This is amazing country. Sea to shining…I'll tell
you what it is. It's fer-tile. I was on my way out the
door one day, little buddy of mine, about to take my
mayoral constitutional, had a handful of pumpkin
seeds to munch on the road. I turn around to wave
goodbye to the wife and kids, and one seed fell outta
my hand. Before I could turn back around that seed
had taken root in the earth, sprouted up and spread
so high and wide that I was dangerously surrounded
by enormous serpentine vines, caught in their green
clutches. The volunteer fire department had to break
out the axes and cut me loose. (*He pauses, remembers…*)
Chuckles? You got a shovel, little buddy? I wanna go
down to the dump, dig up that crocodile.

CHUCKLES: Splish splash?

MAYOR. Listen up now. You can have the head, the tail, and the part in the middle.

(CHUCKLES *thinks, then looks questioningly at the* MAYOR.)

MAYOR. All I wants is the heart. That roll of white fat around the heart of a dragon is good for the pecker. Puts lead in the pencil, woo boy!

CHUCKLES: Dra-gon?

MAYOR. Dragon, crocodile, allygrabber, same thing. You know, little brother, in the spring them dragons fly high and bring the rain. After harvest time they go down and coil in the depths of the sea. Friend of mine rose up to heaven on a red dragon, escorted by blue mice. Right here in town. By the way, you still want to get moving?

(CHUCKLES *nods, looks pleadingly at the* MAYOR.)

MAYOR. Well, you are stupid, but you're not dumb. Listen up. Where you're thinking you maybe wanna be is prob'ly west of here somewheres, you head out past the junction, up by the Shell station, hang a right by the tomb of the Holy Apostle Thomas, pass the railroad yards, left at the tower of Babel and straight on, feet on the whiteline and a smile on your face. Dangerous journey to who knows where. You might be shipwrecked, more than once. Now, if I was you, I'd stick around here a while. You ain't seen nothing here yet. This is interesting country. Look around. Hey…you want a little of this stuff…I brewed some up special for ya.

(MAYOR *takes out flask, gives some to* CHUCKLES…*he drinks…*)

MAYOR. Hey, you gotta get back to work…

(CHUCKLES *remembers his job. He panics, rushes off. Lights up on Karen in her motel room. The* MAYOR *calls after* CHUCKLES.)

MAYOR. Relax. There's the girl in 7. She's not going anywhere, is she? —Not yet. She's waiting.

(KAREN's *room. Liquor bottles, full ashtrays, clothes everywhere. A sudden loud knock at the door. She turns joyfully toward it. It opens, and* CHUCKLES *steps hesitantly inside, his arms full of toilet paper and towels.*)

KAREN: *(Screaming.)* GET OUT!

(CHUCKLES *exits, terrified.* KAREN *shakes out a cigarette, lights it.*)

KAREN: *(V O)* These nights are definitely getting longer. Winter's coming. *(Live)* Fucking ice age. *(V O)* Let's review the facts here, Karen darling. Raised in back of the Hi-Hat Tavern, down the street from Marty's Broiler and the Key Motel. That was a while ago, Karen darling, and now its getting a little late in the afternoon here… *(Live)* I almost got married once. Right out of high school. He dumped me. I had to sit up for two nights picking his name outta my cheerleader jacket. Tick tock. Tick.

(KAREN *turns on her radio. Music. She dances. The* REPORTER *appears in another space. He dances.*)

REPORTER: You dance to this kinda music?

KAREN: *(Live)* Fluently—and we go from there. *(V O)* After a few hours, I notice he's actually listening to what I'm saying, and I say to myself, uh oh Karen girl, here's trouble and I like it. *(Live)* Asshole. God I shoulda just run something on him, taken his money, gone to the ladies, and disappeared. Next day, go shopping. *(V O)* My grandma used to tell me, Karen sweetheart, keep away from cigarette smokers who show up under your window after midnight and play

the banjo. Tick tock. Tick. Pay more attention you
wouldn't end up waiting for someone you hardly
know in some kinda lima bean hell here…Even your
own pain grows boring. *(Live)* Fine. Where we at?
Nighttime. And up above, the stars, little lit windows
of the dead's town, where all the dead sit around being
dead.

Hey, you, Mister Stupid! You don't know what you got
here. You got a full size, moderately fucked up person
here, and I have a lot of potential. What's the matter,
hah? I'm not as good looking as those nineteen year
olds? *(She goes over to the mirror, looks in.)* Bullshit. All
right, some of it's missing, but most of it's there. Are
you aware, Mister Not Here, that I am a model?
(V O) Correction. Was a model. I was sixteen. I did
catalogues. In my last year of high school I did Penny's
for the whole state. *(Live)* I got the pictures. *(V O)* In a
trunk somewheres. Maybe in my mother's house, if she
didn't throw 'em away…

(There's a knock at the door. KAREN *rushes over to answer
it, pulls it open.* CHUCKLES *is standing there again, his arms
full of toilet paper, ready to change the roll. She stares at
him. He doesn't move.)*

KAREN: Come right on in.

*(*CHUCKLES *goes through the room into the bathroom,
strands of toilet paper trailing behind him.)*

KAREN: Care for a cocktail?

*(*CHUCKLES *peers out a moment, looks questioningly at
her, goes back to work.* KAREN *waits for him to leave. He
emerges, and while she's turned away, he leaves a badly
crushed candy bar by her telephone. He walks toward the
door, stops a moment and looks at her.)*

KAREN: Thanks, I guess.

CHUCKLES: *(Mimes wiping his ass and nods vigorously)*
We're easy to get to, but hard to leave. *(He waves
goodbye to her. He exits.)*

KAREN: *(V O)* Where was I? *(Live)* Who the hell knows.
*(She notices the candy bar, picks it up. She looks back toward
the door. V O)* Oh my God…am I that pitiful? *(Live)*
Snickers. Looks like it's been in his pocket in a heat
wave. *(She tosses the crushed candy bar into a corner. V O)*
Three days in this hole. Waiting's just like being dead,
except you still have to pass the time. *(Live. Sings.)*"I
will sing you a song of the New Jerusalem, that far
away home of the soul…" *(V O)* That's all I remember.
(Live) Facts. He's late, *(V O)* he's very late, *(Live)* but
he's on his way, knowing I'd wait forever, that I'd be
here… *(V O)* …staring out the window for him till my
eyes become two tiny swamps where moss floats, till
my lips are food for crows, till deep in the grass grown
up through this crumbling floor, my white bones rot.
(Live) Fuck that. Hell, he'll probably show up any
minute, with a hard-on and a mouth full of sorry. *(A
moment's silence)* You know, after a while, you wait
long enough, you say to yourself, well, actually, this is
it. This is my life. Not what's gonna happen, but now.
I'm here.

*(KAREN is still. Lights come up on FABER and PAULINE as
before, in the motel office. PAULINE is reading a book. FABER
sits. In another area, lights up on the REPORTER. He's
walking through a field: mud, trees. He carries a camera,
notebook. He stops, turns to the audience.)*

REPORTER: I'm free-lance. I take what I can get. My cur-
rent employers, an association of screwballs known
as Flying Saucer News, has been running me into
the ground. I been over half the state in the last three
days. Three days. Damn. I gotta remember the name
of that motel I left her in so's I can call. I been trying,
but it won't come to me. I can find it, I know the

town… Hell, she'll be there. She could tell I was…you know, sometimes you get another chance. You think you'll never get another chance, and God gives you another chance. I'm gonna need some loving after this ring of loons I been chasing. The job? Photo stories on 3 reported sightings. First one was a group of housewives who claimed they witnessed the levitation of an entire shopping mall by alien beings. If that sounds like one valium too many—check. Number two was a Mex ranchhand who was shearing sheeps up country, and got taken aboard a big one. Got him up there stripped naked as a chicken and put him in a room. He claims they wanted him for breeding purposes. I expect he had a real vivid dream out on the prairie. Number three? This one's an ex-professor, lives in the farmhouse up ahead. Once I finish with him, it's pick up Karen, and hit the road…

(The REPORTER *turns away, continues walking as lights dim on him, brighten on* FABER *and* PAULINE *in the motel office. The radio plays quietly.)*

FABER: Pauline, would you…could you sing me a song?

PAULINE: *(Laughs)* I can't sing.

FABER: That's a lie, Pauline.

PAULINE: O K. I won't. You wouldn't want to hear it, Mister Faber, believe me.

FABER: You're wrong there, Pauline. I'd like it.

PAULINE: I don't know any songs.

FABER: You must know one song, Pauline, the one you learned in the third grade, where everybody stood in a row. Sing it, and I'll be sitting here much happier, I think.

PAULINE: I'm not responsible for your happiness, Mister Faber.

FABER: Yes you are, Pauline, and I'm responsible for yours.

(A silence)

PAULINE: We didn't stand in a row. We sat in a circle.

(FABER reaches over and turns off the radio.)

(PAULINE sings, very quietly and simply)

PAULINE: Down in the valley, valley so low
Late in the evening, hear the train blow
Roses love sunshine, violets love dew
Angels in heaven, know I love you
Down in the meadow, down on my knees

Praying to heaven, give my heart ease
Give my heart ease, love, give my heart ease
Praying to heaven, give my heart ease…
That's all I know.

(FABER applauds solemnly.)

PAULINE: Are you making fun of me?

FABER: I am extremely serious here, Pauline.

PAULINE: Good, cause I'd like you to consider something, Mister Faber. This conversation is not just your conversation with me. This is our conversation, Mister Faber, and now it's your turn. Sing.

FABER: I can't sing, Pauline.

PAULINE: That's what I said, Mister Faber.

(FABER, with much hesitancy, begins to sing some romantic ballad— [actor's choice] —poorly. He stops.)

FABER: *(Sings much louder, and begins to bang on the chair in rhythm.)*
Let's twist again, like we did last summer
Yeah, let's twist again, like we did last year
Do you remember when, we were really humming
C'mon, let's twist again, twisting time is here…

PAULINE: Shhhh… You'll wake everybody up.

FABER: All the customers are wide awake, Pauline. One is upstairs walking the floor, and the other one is me. *(He stands, and twists, along with very loud singing.)*
Round and round and up and down we goooooo again
Baby let me know, you love me so, and then…
Let's twist again, like we…

PAULINE: STOP!

(FABER stops singing abruptly.)

FABER: What kind of lipstick is that you got on, Pauline? Flamingo pink? Tangerine blush?

PAULINE: I'm not wearing any lipstick.

FABER: What kind of perfume you wearing? Lily of the Valley? Tiger Musk? Orange Blossom Special?

PAULINE: I'm not wearing any perfume.

FABER: I smell something, Pauline.

PAULINE: Maybe it's my shampoo.

FABER: Answer me something, Pauline. What kind of shampoo?

PAULINE: Apple something…with keratin, whatever that is. Why are you interested in…

FABER: That's private stuff I'm asking about, Pauline. You buy it in the supermarket, but you rub it right on your body. Have a drink. *(Takes out bottle)*

PAULINE: I think I've had enough.

FABER: The last one…

(PAULINE still refuses. FABER refills his own. The bottle is empty.)

FABER: We got a dead soldier here. *(He drops the bottle in the trash.)*

PAULINE: You know, Mister Faber, I've been thinking about what you said, about me sort of…doing more. Maybe moving away to a bigger place or something. I mean, if my Mom is…

FABER: Don't blame me, Pauline.

PAULINE: Blame you?

FABER: One day ten years from now you're lying face down on a cot in some furnished room, crying into your pillow—and you remember. It was me told you to leave the bosom of your home and family. You hurry down to Woolworth's and buy one of those fat black magic markers and you go out to the graveyard and write insulting remarks all over my lily-white headstone.

PAULINE: That's an ugly story. And it's a lie. You won't be dead in ten years, and I won't be in a room somewhere, crying.

FABER: You know the future, Pauline? Should hang a sign on your desk, LIFE READING, TEN BUCKS. You got gypsy blood?

PAULINE: I don't know. May be.

FABER: Maybe you do. *(Silence)* You know, Pauline, I am convinced that for miles around, at this moment, we are the only creatures with their eyes open. The little raccoons and squirrels and stuff in the woods, they're all sleeping, and the people too, all snug in their beds, whole sky over the town is thick with dreams…

PAULINE: *(Looks at her watch)* Mister Mason opens the Snack Shop by the Trailways stop by six, so he's probably up now. And Dexter. He drew the graveyard shift this month, so he's…

FABER: Pauline? I'd like to mention something here. It doesn't matter who the fuck is actually awake, or asleep, or dead, I'm talking about a feeling.

PAULINE: I'm talking about the facts.

FABER: You getting a little sarcastic here, Pauline?

PAULINE: Yes. You've been confusing me, Mister Faber. And scaring me…a little.

FABER: I don't want to do that. I didn't mean to do that. *(A silence)* We're a bunch of poor bastards here, Pauline. Roam the planet like starving dogs, and never get it right. Find any little scrap of something in this world and it's thank God and step careful, cause you're likely to lose that too.
You spend a lot of nights talking to the itinerant sleepers, Pauline. The sleepwalkers. Whatta they have to say on the subject?

PAULINE: You're the only one who ever…

FABER: Maybe you don't hear them cause your pretty head falls over and you sleep at the desk, and all the storytellers can't bear to wake you, so they keep it to themselves and tiptoe by.

PAULINE: I don't think so, Mister Faber. Sometimes I do get sleepy, but I always wake myself, cause what if a car pulls in, and I'm sleeping with my head on the desk, like this. *(Does so)* How does that look, to someone coming in, I mean?

FABER: I don't know. Looks all right to me.

PAULINE: *(Sitting up)* It does not. I do all kinds of things to keep awake. Homework, the radio… You know, sometimes I just think about what might happen to me…if I'll ever get married, or even finish college and find some kind of interesting job. I think about my Mom, and start feeling sad for her and all. Then sometimes I go outside and sit in one of those lawn chairs in front of the office and just wait for it to get light. It happens real slow, so you have to slow yourself down to it or you get bored, cause it takes a few hours. When the first edge of the sun is up, I go back inside and make coffee. It can get real cold out there. Once I did that in the snow. I just kept shaking it off me, and walking around to get warm. I couldn't really tell when the sun came up. The snow was dirty gray in the dark and became white. The sky just got lighter and lighter—till it was light. *(She glances over to a corner, then jumps suddenly.)* Oooooh! Did you see it?

FABER: What?

PAULINE: A mouse. I'm sure I saw a… There it goes!

(Suddenly CHUCKLES bursts into the room, a broom raised over his head. He's trying wildly to kill the mouse or drive it away.)

CHUCKLES: Meece! No!

(Suddenly, CHUCKLES sprawls to the floor. He stares around him desperately. Silence. The mouse seems to be gone. FABER silently points into a corner. The Mouse! CHUCKLES is up, and rushing after it, swinging the broom wildly.)

PAULINE: Chuckles! Stop! Don't hurt it!

(CHUCKLES doesn't hear PAULINE in his passion. He corners the mouse, and energetically smashes it.)

CHUCKLES: Meece! Little meece! No! *(He holds up the dead mouse by the tail. He speaks to it.)* We're easy to get to, but hard to leave!

(CHUCKLES pockets the dead mouse, and exits. FABER looks after him.)

FABER: You know, this place looks ordinary from the outside…

(PAULINE laughs.)

FABER: You ever feel there's strange things going on here .

PAULINE: Strange things? Like a mouse? Or us talking?

FABER: I don't know. *(A long silence)* Last few weeks,
I've seen a lot of dreams with my eyes open, just riding
down the road. I drive through these towns, one after
the other, and they all got a main street, and on it is
a place to buy groceries, Food Town—a place to eat,
Marv's Broiler and a place to get fucked-up, Hi-Hat
Tavern. And when you go through these places in
America, the question is always "Anybody home?"
The answer is obvious. No. Basically, there is nobody
home in America, Pauline. Except you.
But there are people out there, after all. They go way
back, and they came outta the sky and the dirt, just like
us. And they got secrets, just like us. Right now, at this
moment, in this town, everybody's waking up in their
beds, eyes pop open, night still outside the window,
and they rise up, and dress. There they go. There's
the mailman scampering along Main Street, and the
delivery boy, and the girl who works the check-out
counter, and old Mister Mason, slipping outta that
ranchhouse. There's another, behind the Shell station,
and there's another in the river, in an ivory boat being
hauled by a pair of huge catfish, past great green lily
pads awash with flames, and there's your Mom in
a red dress dancing across the village green, all of
them crawling and prancing and snorting towards
the woods outside of town, to a clearing in a ring of
trees. They're out there, under the moon. Rumble and
bumble in the dark! Hop down! Jump up! Spin around,
and old Mister Mason and a teenage girl from the high
school whirl round and round in the center, naked as
jay-birds, and his fat belly wheezes in and out with
the pipes… Know that tune? *(Sings)* O beautiful, for
spacious skies, for amber…waves… Look! They're all
calling to you, Pauline, calling for you to join them. But
you're here talking to Faber, and you forgot. They all
got their party hats on, Pauline, and you're the only
one whose head is bare. Go on. I'll mind the store.

PAULINE: There's no one out there, Mister Faber.
They're home in bed.

FABER: Maybe so, Pauline. Maybe so.

(FABER *and* PAULINE *are quiet. Lights up on the*
PROFESSOR'*s house in the woods, somewhere in America.*
Piles of books and papers, some of which are in cartons.
Strange electronic equipment. Arcane maps and charts.
A telephone. The Professor is packing. The Reporter is
approaching. He stops, turns to the audience.)

REPORTER: Funny. The closer I get to this professor's
place, the stranger I feel, sort of gloomy and nervous
at once, like I'm coming down off something... Hell,
maybe it's the air, seems kinds damp or... Well! Here
we are.

(*A dog howls, loudly and suddenly, unnerving the*
REPORTER *for a moment.*)

REPORTER: Coming along? Let's see how the old duck is
doing. Yoo hoo! Anybody home?

(*The* PROFESSOR *unlocks his door, opens it a crack. Perhaps*
strange atonal music begins, softly.)

PROFESSOR: (*Loud*) Did you bring the pizza? You from
Pizza Hut?

REPORTER: (*After hesitating*) You order a large
pepperoni with anchovies and a diet coke?

PROFESSOR: Exactly. Come in, come in.

(*The* REPORTER *enters, and the* PROFESSOR *quickly shuts*
the door and locks it behind him.)

REPORTER: Professor, why we playing charades?

PROFESSOR: Act normally, please. All your questions
will be answered in time. (*He nervously looks out the*
window, then back to the room.) You are from Flying
Saucer News?

REPORTER: Yeah. You know something? I just remembered the name of a motel I gotta call. Can I use your phone?

PROFESSOR: I told you in my letter. To the magazine. I don't have a phone.

REPORTER: *(Pointing to the phone)* What's that? A ding-dong school phone?

PROFESSOR: The wires are down. They haven't come to repair them in months. They get too many flat tires.

REPORTER: What the hell are you talking about?

(Loud noises from outside. CHUCKLES bursts into the room, panicked and upset. The body of a dog, wrapped in a bloody towel, is in his arms.)

CHUCKLES: Dead dog. *(The Professor puts an arm around Chuckles' shoulder to comfort him…)*

PROFESSOR: Bury him in the garden. Next to the other one. I'll write the pound. This time, we'll get a dog so big that… *(To the REPORTER)* This is Chuckles. He helps around the place. Chuckles, this is the man from the magazine.

(CHUCKLES and the REPORTER shake hands awkwardly. To CHUCKLES:)

PROFESSOR: Keep packing!

(CHUCKLES exits. To REPORTER:)

PROFESSOR: Shouldn't you be taking notes?

REPORTER: My memory's sharp as a tack, profesor.

PROFESSOR: Where were we?

REPORTER: Let's see if I have this right. You said in your letter that some kind of invisible creatures are out there in the woods, and you been talking to them.

PROFESSOR: In a word, yes.

REPORTER: If we could see them, what would they look like?

PROFESSOR: Like men…and women.

REPORTER: And you think they're from earth? Or Mars? Or outer space?

PROFESSOR: They come originally from the place of broken shells, a great sea of psychic debris from previous worlds, worlds that failed…a sort of spiritual version of the asteroid belt.

REPORTER: O K. Moving right along. You might as well hit me with the rest of it.

PROFESSOR: *(Pause)* The rest of it is…less theoretical.

I left the doors open, so they could go freely, in and out. I was friendly, genial. They liked Chuckles. I won them over. They came when I called, drifting out of the woods. They guided me, taught me… A man should marry for love. Don't you think so, Mister Reporter?

REPORTER: I know so.

PROFESSOR: I did. I married one of them. A woman of the shadow people. I loved her as I'd never been able to love one of us. She was devoted, at first, but she became unruly. Sexually demanding. She behaved badly. I couldn't help it. I had to…

REPORTER: Go on…

PROFESSOR: I locked her in the closet. She's extremely clever. She escaped, and fled back to them. They were furious. They told me to leave at once. Their speech, by the way, is a kind of gurgling, like a brook over stones. These last few days, they grow more malicious. She has inflamed them against me. They wait around the house, in the trees.

You know, she never really loved me.

I have to leave here. I'm a pauper. I'm unemployable.
Perhaps I'll be hospitalized. But I must go. You see,
they'll kill me. I know they will. I have to tell the
truth before they stop me. They explain everything.
Parapsychology, mental illness, war, religion. The
whole banana. They don't want their secrets known.
Would you? Are you frightened?

REPORTER: No.

PROFESSOR: You should be. You can't hurt them, you
know. And they won't die.

REPORTER: Why don't you just apologize to your…
wife? For locking her in the closet. Make it up to her.
Let them know you…

PROFESSOR: She was wicked. She deserved punishment.
You don't believe any of this, do you? *(He goes over to a
tape recorder.)* Proof positive! Their voices…

(The PROFESSOR *presses "Play". The sound of a loud harsh
bubbling and gurgling fills the room. Then suddenly the tape
recorder begins to smoke, then bursts into flames.)*

PROFESSOR: Damn them. You want more proof?
Wait here.

*(*CHUCKLES *enters with a pile of papers in his hands.)*

PROFESSOR: Talk to Chuckles. He may be insane, but
he's not dumb.

(The PROFESSOR *Exits.* CHUCKLES *stares at the Reporter.)*

REPORTER: What the hell is going on here?

*(*CHUCKLES *begins packing.)*

REPORTER: You all nuts or something? Look, I can take
a joke, but…

CHUCKLES: Go away. Go!

REPORTER: What's going on?

(CHUCKLES *picks up some scattered papers, rushes out of the room as the* PROFESSOR *returns, holding a large plaster cast, with some odd markings on it.)*

PROFESSOR: Their marks. Proof positive.

REPORTER: That could be a plaster cast of anything. A child could have made those prints, or you, or a tree branch, or…anything could have done this.

PROFESSOR: Anything didn't. The shadow people did.

REPORTER: I can't take anymore of this. There's a visible woman waiting for me in a motel room, and I got to get back to her before she disappears. Goodbye, Professor, and good luck.

PROFESSOR: *(Barring his way)* NO! Listen to me. Please. Write the story. Besides, you can't go. Out there, in the mood they're in, they may hurt you…or worse. They don't like the light as well as the dark. Wait until morning.

REPORTER: You should get some kind of help, you know that?

PROFESSOR: I know that. You are the help I was hoping to get.

REPORTER: I'm leaving.

PROFESSOR: It's your life.

REPORTER: Yeah. It is.

PROFESSOR: Chuckles! Let him out.

(CHUCKLES *appears, unlocks the door for the* REPORTER, *who exits.* CHUCKLES *watches him go. The* PROFESSOR *turns away. A scream from outside. The* PROFESSOR *rushes to the window. The curtains stir in a sudden wind. They both stare out in panic, then slowly turn away.)*

PROFESSOR: They've killed him. His body is lying there…

*(In the distance, what could be the sound of a car, or the wind, or...*CHUCKLES *listens.)*

CHUCKLES: *(Mimes driving)* Brummmmmmmmm. Brummmmmmmmmmm.

PROFESSOR: No. That sound—the shadow people crying to each other in the trees… They'll rush the house, I know it. Quick, Chuckles, the evidence!

*(*CHUCKLES *hands* PROFESSOR *the plaster cast.)*

PROFESSOR: Distract them while I run for it. They won't hurt you. Noises! *(He grabs the reel of tape off the recorder.)* Now!

*(*CHUCKLES, *frightened, begins to bang his hands together, stamp his feet, make whatever noise he can.)*

PROFESSOR: Goodbye.

(The PROFESSOR *rushes out the door, leaving it open behind him. He's gone.* CHUCKLES *remains, making noise, hopping up and down in fear and panic. An electric flash, and the lights go out.* CHUCKLES's *noise stops for a moment. Then it resumes in the darkness, louder and fiercer than before. It continues, and fades, as lights come up on* KAREN's *motel room. She is holding a pad and pencil.)*

KAREN: *(V O, reading what she's written.)* "If you ever read this, that means you came back, and I'd already left. You think I'd wait around to…" *(Crosses out, writes)* "You can reach me at…" *(Crosses out, writes)* "Leave a message for me at the …" *(Crosses out, writes)* "My mom's phone number is 857-6621. I'll call there every day to see if you…" *(She stops writing. Live)* He'll never see this. *(She crumples up the note and throws it in a corner. V O)* Now how'm I gonna make it outta this hole. Paying the tab and leaving like a lady is out of the question. *(She begins to pack her suitcase. Live)* Without all this shit I could smile at the girl at the desk, say I'm getting some very fresh air, and hit the highway—but

I am taking my worldly possessions. I got a blouse in there I haven't even worn yet. *(V O)* O K. Downstairs, suitcase in hand, deal with the girl at the desk, and hope she doesn't reach for the phone.

(CHUCKLES, *in another space, dim light, listening.)*

KAREN: *(Live)* "Listen, Pauline, honey, I got in a bind. This can happen to a girl sometimes and if you don't know it yet, you will. Now I didn't find a window and stiff the place, did I? I'm right here in front of you. And you know why I'm standing here? The cops? I'd be long gone. I don't give a shit about whoever owns this joint. I'm here cause I was concerned about you. If I skipped, it might come outta your salary. I couldn't stand the idea of fucking over another working girl. So what I got to say is this, and I'm saying please. I will send you the money. That's God's own truth. Soon as I get work, I will send you the money for the entire bill. Gimme the bill. I want it. It's got the address on it? Good. Pauline, some day if you hit a rough patch, I hope someone treats you the way you're treating me. Now listen honey, I want you to look at something…

(Lights dim out on CHUCKLES *in the other space.* KAREN *takes a piece of costume jewelry out of her suitcase.)*

KAREN: *(Live)* My mother gave it to me. It's worth a hundred dollars if it's worth a dime. Here. You loan me twenty bucks on it, and when I send in the money for the bill, I'll pay you back and you can… *(V O)* Forget the jewelry bit. The rest might go. It'll work. *(Live)* And if it don't, well, what can they do to me that hasn't already been done? All right. It's time to take my old Granny's advice. *(She gets into bed, sitting up, wide awake.)* When in trouble, pull down the shades and pay a visit to some other town, where the new girl is a pleasing novelty. *(Live and V O)* Karen darling, soon as it's light, we go.

(Lights fade on KAREN. *Lights up on* FABER *and* PAULINE *in the motel office.)*

FABER: Pauline —you think you're worth fighting for? If I was with you, I mean, if we were saying all this naked and with my mouth right up against your ear, and a huge gorilla with a baseball bat came up alongside the bed and said Faber get outta there, you gotta fight me first in the parking lot, you think I should just leave—or have it out with him?

PAULINE: Mister Faber, I think maybe you should just relax and stop talking for a little bit. O K?

FABER: Well?

PAULINE: You'd do what you'd do, that's all. Depending.

FABER: Depending on what, Pauline?

PAULINE: A lot of things.

FABER: What things?

PAULINE: Mister Faber, you're thinking about something that wasn't. And isn't. And won't be.

FABER: I got a tendency, Pauline. To do just that. You know, there's a lot of people who think their life is what happens to them. Get a job, get married, eat an ice cream cone. It's a great life.
There's another kind of people who don't connect what happens to them with their lives at all. Their life is something else…hopefully.
Shit. I gotta get out of here. You gonna run out of patience, and I'm gonna run out of money. But—if I just hit the road I'll end up another place like this one, and for places like this one, this one's fine. What do you think, Pauline?

PAULINE: It doesn't matter much, Mister Faber. The question is, what do you think?

FABER: I don't know, Pauline. I truly don't... But hey, I'm trying...

PAULINE: Trying is just trying, Mister Faber. You've got to do something.

FABER: Was that advice, Pauline? Are you telling me how I should...

PAULINE: Just forget it, Mister Faber, O K. I'm just talking. You got me trying to answer you. You know that? I don't even know what I should do.

FABER: Pauline, do you think our life is supposed to be interesting?

PAULINE: Every moment doesn't have to be interesting...but it is.

FABER: For you.

PAULINE: I don't feel sorry for you, Mister Faber. I sort of want to, but I don't. I feel like laughing. Not at you. Just laughing.

(PAULINE *is almost having a fit of the giggles, but manages to stop herself.* FABER *stares at her. They sit quietly, as lights come up on the bar, and the carnival lot. In the bar, the T V is on, picture and low sound.* LINDA *and* TIM *are hanging out, watching the tube. In the lot, same setting as when we saw Bonecrusher: an enclosure, some carnival lights—but the banner of Egypt is gone. The* PITCHMAN, *his hat on, and a suitcase in his hand, is standing where his chair and microphone used to be. He walks away from the carnival slowly, crosses the stage, and is gone. In the bar, the* PROFESSOR *enters, carrying his plaster cast. The reel of audio tape is in his pocket, some hanging out. He looks ragged, his clothes torn in places. He sits at the bar.)*

TIM: Hi. My names's Tim. This is Linda. Linda, say hello to the nice man.

LINDA: Hello.

(Suddenly, the T V image changes to a close-up of the PROFESSOR. *He's on a street somewhere, clearly the interviewee of some sort of local television.)*

PROFESSOR: Turn it up, please. That's me.

*(*TIM *turns up the T V sound.* TIM, LINDA, *and the* PROFESSOR *watch the show.)*

PROFESSOR: *(On T V)* The shadow people are among us. They're around us, all the time. They explain everything. Parapsychology, war, mental illness, religion. They can't control the weather. Or fly. Or raise the dead. They're very light, you know. The wind can blow them away. Very light. Very beautiful. Some say they've always existed, and will exist forever. I wouldn't say that. Some say they…

TIM: *(He reaches up and slaps off the T V. Silence)* Come on, Linda. Let's go.

*(*TIM *exits.* LINDA *follows, but before she leaves, she turns back to the* PROFESSOR *and the audience.)*

LINDA: Goodbye.

*(*LINDA *exits. After a long moment, the* PROFESSOR *moves toward the door as the lights dim on the bar, and on the carnival lot. We return to* FABER *and* PAULINE *as before. A long silence)*

FABER: So. What do you think, Pauline? You think the world's gonna end tonight? Twenty ton hypernuclear bomb drops right through the roof of the motel. We're safe in the eye, sitting here in a great crown of fire, while in the sky, all the dead from all over America, each one a thin paper of ash—and the fire dies, and the wind dies, and they float down from where they been spinning in heaven, drift down slow and easy, doing their last dead dance in the air. Then it's quiet, just you, and me.

(CHUCKLES *Enters, sweeping quietly. Long pause.*) No
comment. O K. So. What do you think, Pauline? You
think we're supposed to be happy here?

PAULINE: At the motel?

FABER: You know what I mean.

PAULINE: I think…we are happy here. That happiness
is another word for our life. That we were made for joy
in everything, even our death.

FABER: Pauline, you hear that in church or somewhere?

PAULINE: No, Mister Faber. I know it. Cause I saw it.

FABER: It's not a thing you can see, Pauline.

PAULINE: You're wrong, Mister Faber…I saw it in my
father's eyes before he died. I was standing there, and
he had all these tubes in him, and he was trying to
speak and no one could make out the words.

(CHUCKLES *approaches them. He listens.*)

PAULINE: He was looking right at me, and then my
Mom went over close to him, and he spoke again.
"What'd he say, Ma?" "He says you're an angel." He
was seeing it, and then I could feel it, like a light all
around me, and him, and my Mom. It sounds terrible
to say, with him so sick and all, but I felt very happy.
He died that night, by himself, while everyone else was
sleeping. A little of that happiness is in me, still. It's a
truer thing than the other ways I feel sometimes—so I
try to…remember.

FABER: It was years ago…couple of months after my
father died, I went to the beach. I was lying there
on the sand, and I saw him. He was rising up out
of the water, but not like some religious painting or
something. He was just walking out of the ocean in his
bathing suit. He always loved swimming in the ocean.
He came in dripping from a calm sea, and walked

over to me. I knew he was dead, and that it was a…
something in my head or… He looked very happy to
see me there. He smiled, and waved—and that little
moment made me feel he loved me in a way nothing
in his life had ever done…and that was it. Then he was
gone, and I was smiling, almost laughing, and the tears
were running down my face.

(A silence. CHUCKLES *rings the desk bell once. He moves
away from them slowly, and exits.)*

FABER: You ever think about dying, Pauline?

PAULINE: I've thought about it, but not all the time or
anything. I've got enough…

FABER: One world at a time, right, Pauline?

(The phone rings. PAULINE *picks it up.)*

PAULINE: *(On phone)* Office…we have one guest who
might be who you're looking for…I'll connect you. *(She
puts the call through, hangs up. To* FABER.*)* The girl in
seven. She got a call. Goes to show.

FABER: Goes to show what?

PAULINE: Goes to show that…if I say, you'll say "you
learn that in church or something, Pauline?"

FABER: Well?

PAULINE: Well, what?

FABER: Well, you gonna marry me or not, Pauline?

PAULINE: You didn't ask me, Mister Faber.

FABER: I'm asking you now.

PAULINE: No.

FABER: O K. Unrequited love, that's O K. Better than no
love at all. And I'll know you're here, Pauline. Right in
the middle of America, like a fountain of snow.

(A long silence)

PAULINE: How much longer are you gonna be staying, Mister Faber?

FABER: You know something, Pauline. I better leave in the morning...I better go home, wherever that is. Keep the porch light on, Momma. Let it shine out onto the lawn, and don't turn it off till sunrise, cause that's when I'm coming. There, that's me, little plume of dust rising, that's me in the dust cloud, coming from the east, with the sun behind me in splendour...hey, who knows? So. What do you think, Pauline?

PAULINE: I don't know, Mister Faber. What do you think?

(FABER and PAULINE are still. CHUCKLES appears, and alongside him, the MAYOR. Lights come up as well on all the other places we've seen: KAREN's room, the bar, the carnival lot, the PROFESSOR's house, the open field.)

MAYOR. Interesting country, little buddy. You lucky you here.

(The MAYOR steps back into darkness, as lights fade on all places. CHUCKLES alone. Light fades on CHUCKLES, and out.)

END OF PLAY

PRODUCTION NOTE

The set for AMERICAN NOTES is basically six places: motel reception area; Karen's motel room; Pitchman's banner and showfront; Professor's house; Tim and Linda's bar; and the Mayor's area. Where these are in relation to each other, and whether all the areas are onstage all the time are questions that I hope would be answered by each individual production according to its needs and interests.

The settings in a particular production can be very full and realistic places—or sparse theatrical arrangements that indicate the nature of place through significant objects. We should have the feeling that a great dark sky is overhead.

The music is all American music, and can range from rock and roll to muzak to country and western.

Please leave space in the language, and between the people, for silence.

It is night, we are in America, and the time is now.

9 780881 456165